SMILES
David McEnery

Smiles

A collection of
humorous photographs
by David McEnery

A Mirror Group Book

Design : Chris Spencer

© 1975 David McEnery/Rex Features Limited.
© 1975 This collection Mirror Group Newspapers Limited
Published by Mirror Group Books,
79 Camden Road, Camden, London, NW1 9NT.
Printed in Great Britain by A.B.C. Printers, Storrington, Sussex.

ISBN 0 85939 053 5

Introduction

"When I don't know whether to laugh o
cry," says David McEnery, "I try to laug
It's the only way to stay sane."

He looks at you with a twinkle in h
green eyes, adding: "And it's the on
way to stay solvent."

For David McEnery has turned h
philosophy of life into a means of earnin
his living. Not only does he try to see th
funny side of every situation, but he wi
often photograph it. And it is thes
pictures that have won him fame an
(relative) fortune as the world's funnie:
photographer.

The McEnery world, as detailed in h:
crisp black and white pictures, is simila
to ours, but funnier. The scenes an
settings may be familiar, but there i
always some detail or difference i
emphasis that transforms them from th
ordinary to the amusing.

In his world cars can sprout legs an
walk, parking meters can get themselve
knotted (as urged by many a motorist) an
guard dogs can drive security vans.

It is a world that seems to contain mor
fat ladies than average. More bare
bummed kids and more nubile beautie:
Music is supplied by a three-legge
banjo player, and there is even a ma
whose head floats along two feet behin
his shoulders.

The geographical location of this worl
is no secret. It is Brighton, where Davi
has lived for the last 20 years.

Visitors will find little that is intrinsicall
comic in this charming seaside town. O:
the contrary, it exudes an air of gentee
respectability – a legacy from Regenc
days when London's high society flocke
to enjoy its sea breezes and wide prom
enades.

The only hint of the bizarre is given b
the famous Dome, the folly designed b

he Prince Regent as a rival to the world's most esoteric architecture. Actually it looks more like a set for a Hollywood version of the Arabian Nights.

You will look in vain for double-deck pushchairs or three-legged banjoists.

The truth is that the Brighton of David McEnery is in the eye of the beholder – or, in this case, the lens of a unique photographer. The comedy is there, all right; but it takes a special eye – a McEnery eye – to see it.

Some of his pictures may appear surreal or impossible. Closer inspection, however, often reveals the explanation. That "headless" man is simply carrying a mirror on his shoulder; that walking car is a shell being carried to a car dump.

Other pictures in this collection draw their humour from a unique perception of the occasional silliness of the human animal. A fat lady vainly hopes to reduce her weight by lifting one foot off the weighing machine; a boyfriend finds a fully-clothed busty stranger more alluring than his own dolly, who is equally busty . . . and topless.

We, the public, are the actors in these comic cameos. The photographer is not poking fun at us. He is inviting us to laugh at ourselves.

In a world that gets less funny every day, David's pictures can remind us of this most vital of human gifts – our sense of humour. And it really is a *vital* gift, for it helps us cope with life. Most of us are so preoccupied with our daily worries that we never take a really close look at ourselves. We are blind to the humour of our situation; we take ourselves too seriously.

"Stop, step back and look," is the message of David's work. "You have to laugh."

David was born in Walsall, Staffs, "Just over 35 years ago" as he says. Creativity must run in his family, for his two younger brothers Peter and John are both highly successful actors.

David has always been a press photographer. When he moved to Brighton 20 years ago he began working on local papers in the area. "I always did look for the funny slant in pictures. Then one day I offered a funny to a national paper. They bought it on the spot." That was when he decided to leave the *Brighton Argus* and go freelance.

It had never occurred to him that a living was to be had from humour alone. And it hadn't occurred to most editors of national papers either, some of whom at first greeted his work with disdain.

But in time it was realised that the McEnery view of life was an ideal antidote to the predominant gloom of hard news. Next to pretty girls, there is nothing like a laugh to help you start the day. In his 15 years as a freelance working for the nationals, David has not only earned a fair living, but has established a new category of newspaper picture. He likes to call it "photographic cartooning".

David has been married twice and has two children. In celebration of his second divorce he photographed his "Just Divorced" picture, a new twist on an old theme.

"I don't necessarily find divorce a funny subject," he says. "But that was one of those occasions when I didn't know whether to laugh or cry."

David McEnery is exclusively handled by Rex Features Ltd., who have placed his work in publications all over the world.

Swing high. It can be dicey when steel-erectors get dozey. Nodding off could mean signing off for good. But here's a man who brought a little ingenuity to the problem. He strung his hammock in the scaffolding high above Brighton. Now he can take a lunch-time snooze instead of climbing to the ground and back.

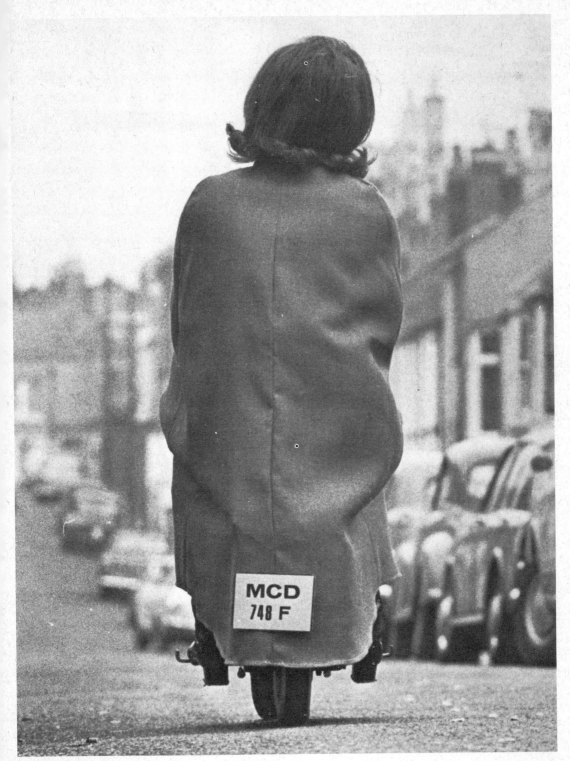

Capability King. A capable girl is Susie King. She likes to keep her mini-scooter as smart as herself. That's how she came to design this amazing maxi-cape. It fits easily over both girl and scooter. And the number plates add a legalising touch.

Royal flush. A convenient throne for a game of poker. Fred the carpenter and his mates are enjoying their lunchtime flutter. And it looks as if Fred really is sitting pretty! A royal flush, no less!

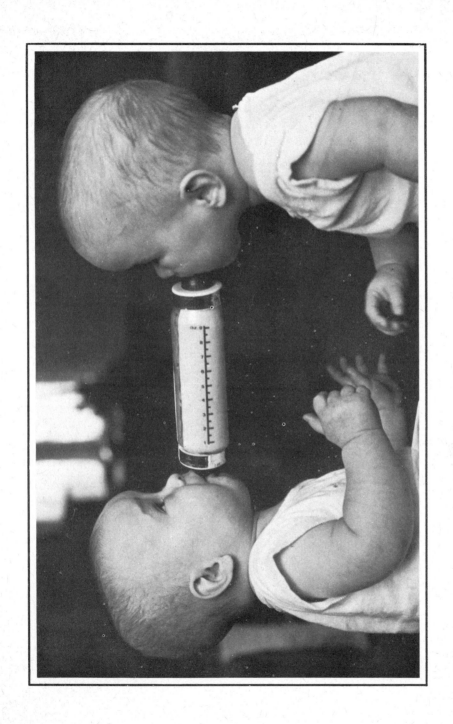

Travelling light. Keeping cool is no problem for Emma Rippon. When you are only two public nudity is quite acceptable. She is flying with her family to St. Tropez, where her topless-bottomless look will be a sensation.

1. "Halt, Madam, if you don't mind," says PC Jock Mackintosh. Little Emma, aged two, does just that. From her level the PC presents a towering obstacle, not to be argued with.

2. "There's nothing wrong, Madam," soothes the constable, and sweeps Emma, car and all, into his arms. "But you must be careful and not drive too close to the road." His finger wags in mock severity.

3. And just to show there's no hard feelings, he plants a big kiss on her cheek. Emma is overawed. Not that she minds being kissed . . . but oh, those whiskers!

Doggone? Oh, those long, passionate kisses! Enough to make a man forget time, forget his excuse for coming to the park. Could it be he was supposed to be walking the dog? If so, this dog has wandered off to do his own courting.

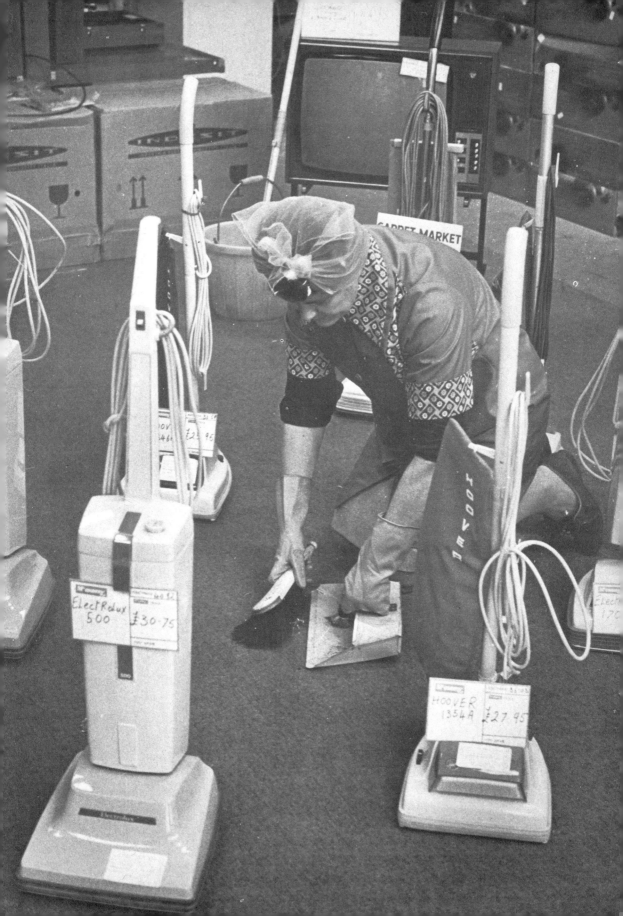

No fuel like an old fuel. A meeting of past and present. But the easy rider doesn't feel smug. The juice he puts in his mount can cost a week's wages. Water, on the other hand, is still almost free.

A stitch in time. "Eyes right, Dad! Such blatant baring of bosoms could never have happened in our day. I really don't know what to make of it." Dad knows what to make of it. But it's hard to see past Mum's knitting. Niki Pauwels, a 19-year-old Parisienne, doesn't notice the excitement she is causing.

Brolly dolly. Attractive girls often need both hands free. Especially when they are carrying home the shopping and it starts to rain. Handling an umbrella then can be a laugh—for everyone else. This variation of a brolly needs no holding, but perches securely on the shoulders.

Walking in, please pass. What with the price of petrol these days it's often cheaper to walk. And it looks as if these two are trying to get the best of both worlds. Housewife Penny Holden sold her beat-up mini for spares. But nobody wanted the shell. With the help of a neighbour, Penny had to walk it to the scrapyard.

Bathrooms

DOGS MUST
BE CARRIED

DOGS MUS
BE CARRIEI

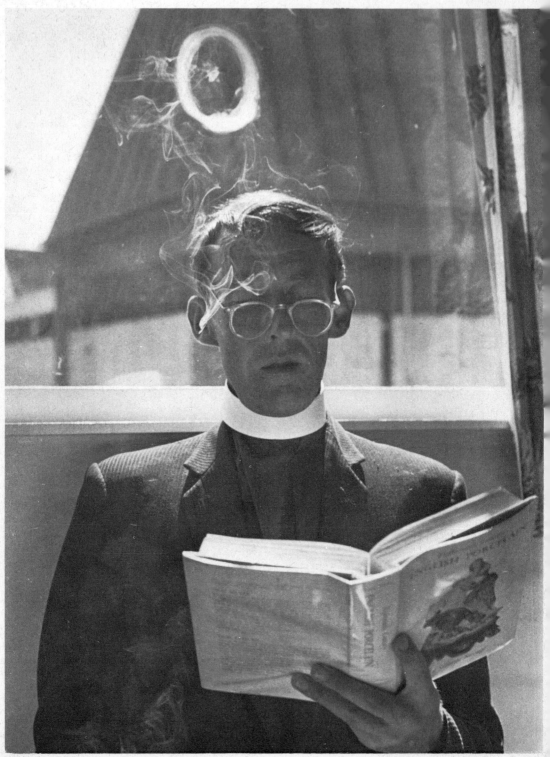

Holy smoke. It's miraculous what the camera can do. This Hastings vicar was enjoying a quiet cigarette, a casual smoke ring drifted up—and the camera clicked. "Holy smoke!" whispered the photographer.

Econo-mini. It goes like clockwork. This spring-driven mini could be the answer to the world fuel crisis. But it's only a giggle. Some student joker at Brighton Technical College is just trying to wind us all up . . .

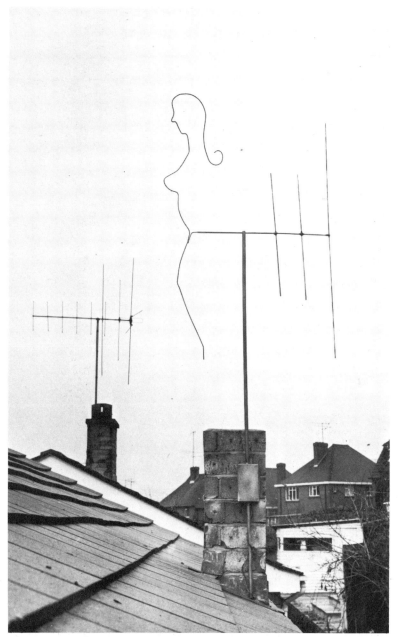

TV Topper. This TV aerial used to be as square as the next man's. But it got bent when engineer Mick Arnett was fixing it . . . and he decided to finish the job with a little artistic licence. Reception, we hear, is better than ever.

Sonshade. When Mum is the dolly-bird type a son gets used to being left in the shade. And this little lad doesn't resent it. For his ingenious Mum has designed the perfect sonshade. It's a neat way to avoid sonburn . . . and Mumburn too.

The budget bride. All seemed lost when the photographer's car broke down. The best man, though, had an idea. With little time left before the honeymoon train left from Brighton station, he rushed the happy couple into the photos-while-you-wait booth. Two minutes later they had the strangest pictures ever. But all's well . . .

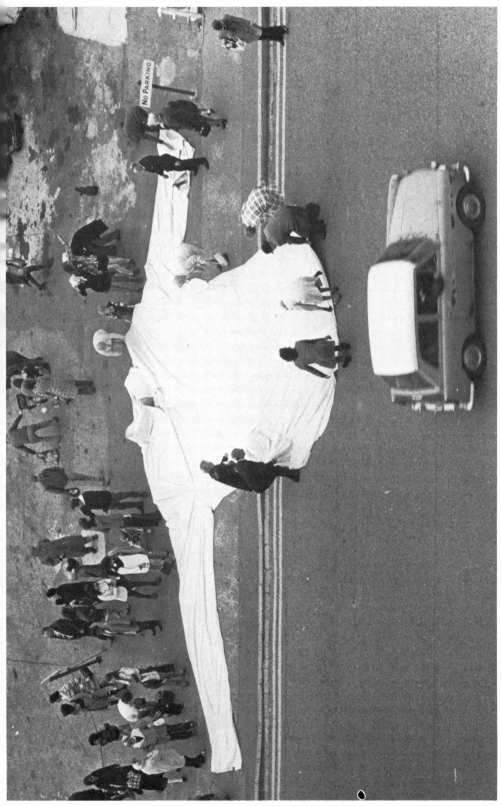

One of Gulliver's garments? Not one of Gulliver's cast-offs, but still the largest shirt in the world. It took seven maids seven days to make it. It was the main attraction at a cancer research benefit fete and certainly drew the crowds. On Brighton beach forty intrigued holidaymakers helped spread it out for the camera.

Brighton rainy. Sometimes British summers are not sunny. Sometimes, indeed, they are awful. This holidaymaker was anticipating weather of tropical heat. As it was he got the tropical monsoon.

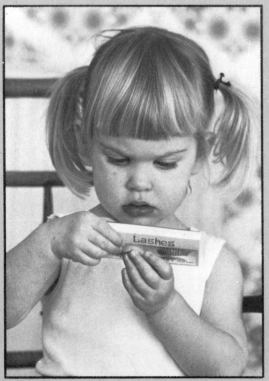

1. "False lashes, just like Mum's."

2. "Let's see—first a lick . . ."

3. "Then plonk on the eye . . ."

4. "Hmmm. It doesn't look right."

84

5. "But the effect is quite cheeky . . ."

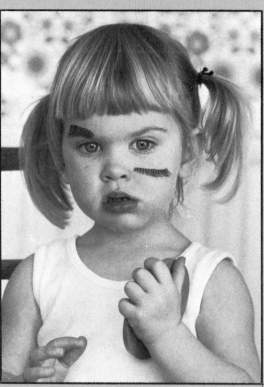

6. "Now the next. Another lick and . . ."

7. "Missed again! But it'll have to do."

8. "A girl hasn't all day to mess about!"

85

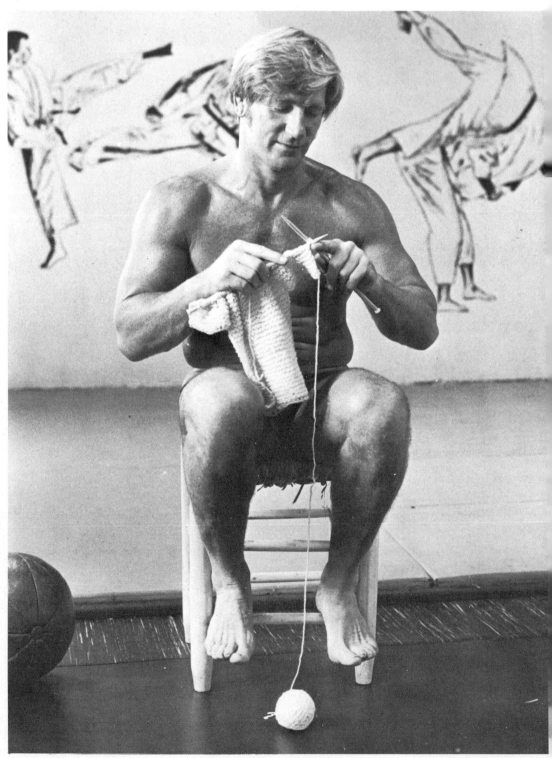

Big knit. Giant Joe Robinson is 6 feet 3 inches of solid muscle, a former heavyweight wrestling champion with a black belt in karate and judo. He used to teach Sean Connery self-defence. These days he could teach him knitting. For Joe is a knitting fanatic. ''It helps my concentration,'' he says.

CASH

MISTAKES CANNOT
BE RECTIFIED LATER

Bovver babe. Engine drivers are out of date. When three-year-old Gerrard Miller grows up he wants to be a skinhead. He already has the haircut and the braces, and he will soon grow into the boots. But by the time this bristletop is big enough, skinheads will be as out of date as Teddy Boys.

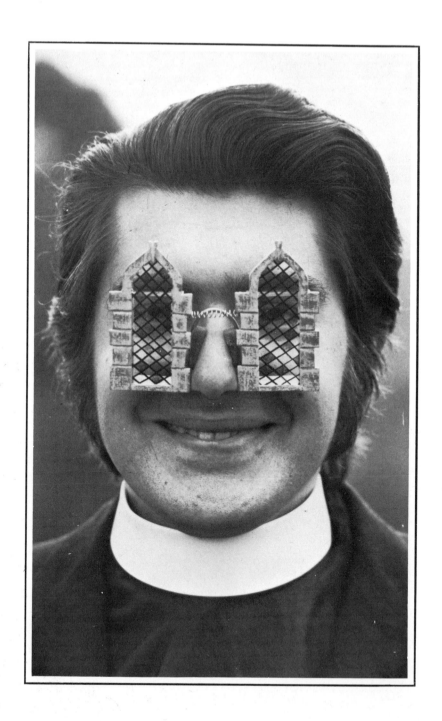

A brief line . . . Model Jenny Stone never forgets the day of the week. She is too well-briefed for that. Jenny is the methodical type, who believes the secret of a well-planned week is to begin at the bottom. Hence each day is marked on the appropriate panties, so there can be no mistake. And Monday is always washday, as you can see

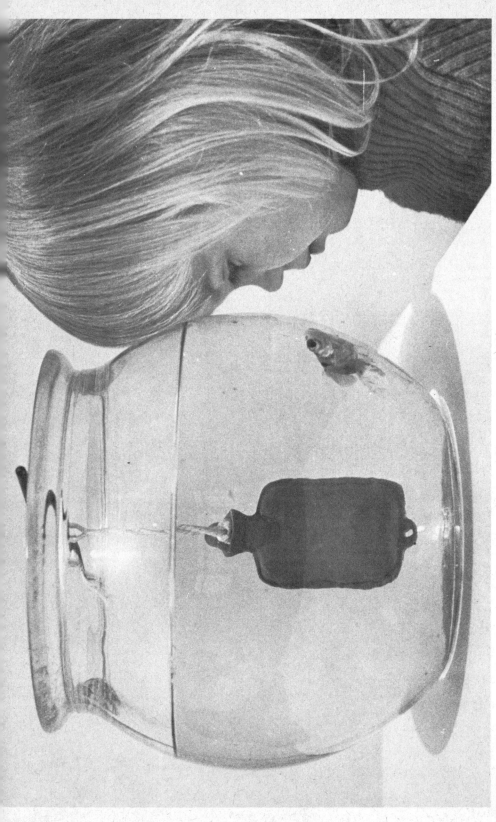

No cold fish. Bubble-eyed Veil Tails feel the cold. It can kill them. That's why Emma is taking every precaution to see that her exotic goldfish stays warm. While the tropical tank is being cleaned, her fish occupies a conventional bowl. And the doll's hot-water bottle keeps the temperature right.

NEWSPAPERS · MAGAZINES
GIRL
PENTHOUSE
MAYFAIR
King
RAVEN
GIRLS of the WORLD
KNAVE
travelling man's edition
MAYFAIR
King
Fiesta

A carakennel for a canine camper. Rusty may be a mongrel, but his holidays fall into the luxury class. His master, Cliff Wilks, loves to take him camping . . . in his own dog-sized caravan. The doghouse on wheels is unique. Ideas as good as this, however, have a habit of catching on.

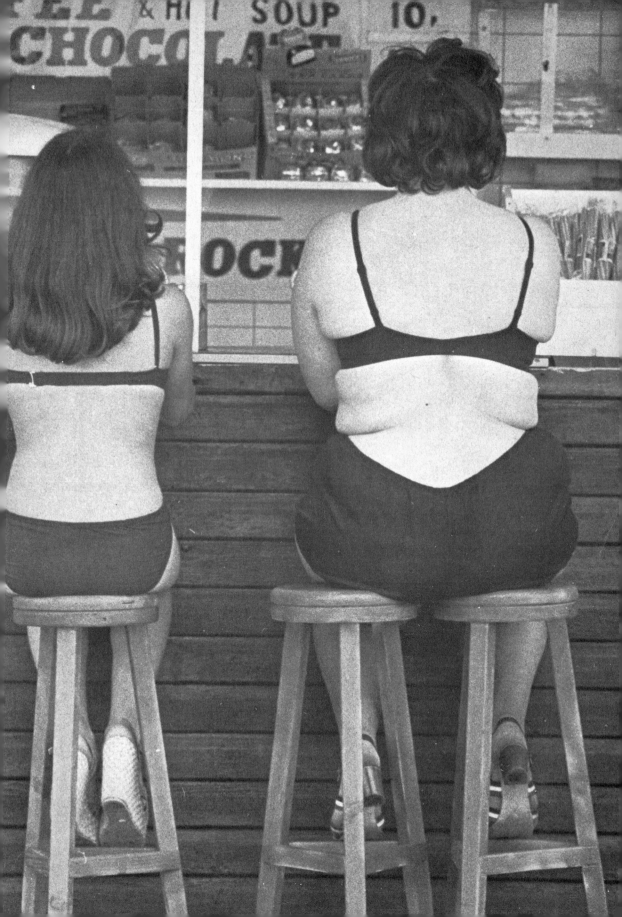

The weigh of all flesh. It's never too early for a girl to start thinking about her figure. Still, this tiny weight watcher has a few years to go before she need worry. Right now the machine means little to her. It's just another of those adult ''pleasures'' she as yet doesn't appreciate.

Weighing yourself can be a depressing experience. This man is finding the awful truth hard to take. Holidays may be a time to loosen your belt and start in on the beer and chips, but this is ridiculous. However, his footsore son may soon throw some light on the subject.

More optimistic is this lady, who is used to reading the gloomy truth of weighing machine dials. Maybe lifting one leg won't improve things, but anything is worth trying. Anything but dieting.

Love is a shared weighing machine. Just halve your total
weight and one of you must feel lighter. In this case passers-
by got more than anyone bargained for, as a dislodged
bikini top revealed a part that doesn't need slimming at all.

How much will it weigh? It's hard to tell like this. But the speculation is exciting. Besides, what woman can resist being able to say: "I may be heavy, but it's not all my fault!"

Oh, Mr Porter! It's that Emma again. Naked again. So long as you have your mask and flippers (and, of course, your socks), who needs a bathing suit? "Which way is the sea?" she asks Mr Porter. But first Mr Porter wants to know where her Daddy is. Spoilsport.

SCHOOL
of YOGA
(2nd floor)

Shake, rattle and roll. Labourer Mick Stepney picks up good vibrations. Those headphones shut out the shattering noise of the drill—and let in sole sweet music from his cassette player.

Not such a scarey-crow. It may scare the crows, but it attracts the men. A market gardener found the birds treated his conventional scarecrow with contempt. Then he found a discarded dressmaker's doll and set it up instead. It worked. And it caused many a passer-by to take a second look.

Dangerous curves. Bottom gear gets a new meaning as Jan Dixon changes into her racing overalls. Model Jan is learning to be a Formula Four driver. And race ace David Purley is her teacher. There are no changing rooms for girls at Goodwood. But Jan's not shy ; and the male drivers don't mind either.